Invisible Journeys
Communication

Caroline Grimshaw

TEXT EDITOR IQBAL HUSSAIN
SCIENCE CONSULTANT JOHN STRINGER

Invisible Journeys
Communication

CREATIVE AND EDITORIAL DIRECTOR
CONCEPT/FORMAT/DESIGN/TEXT
CAROLINE GRIMSHAW

TEXT EDITOR **IQBAL HUSSAIN**
SCIENCE CONSULTANT **JOHN STRINGER**
ILLUSTRATIONS
NICK DUFFY ※ **SPIKE GERRELL**
CAROLINE GRIMSHAW
THANKS TO
TIM SANPHER COMPUTER IMAGERY
LAURA CARTWRIGHT PICTURE RESEARCH
BRONWEN LEWIS EDITORIAL SUPPORT

TITLES IN THIS SERIES ⟶ ※ SUN
※ COMMUNICATION

CONCEIVED AND DESIGNED BY CAROLINE GRIMSHAW FOR
TWO-CAN PUBLISHING LTD
346 OLD STREET
LONDON EC1V 9NQ

FIRST PUBLISHED BY TWO-CAN PUBLISHING LTD IN 1997
IN ASSOCIATION WITH FRANKLIN WATTS

HARDBACK ISBN 1-85434-445-5
PAPERBACK ISBN 1-85434-446-3
DEWEY DECIMAL CLASSIFICATION 384

HARDBACK 2 4 6 8 10 9 7 5 3 1
PAPERBACK 2 4 6 8 10 9 7 5 3 1

A CATALOGUE RECORD FOR THIS BOOK IS AVAILABLE
FROM THE BRITISH LIBRARY.

PRINTED IN HONG KONG.

I am your Route Maestro. I will show you the way.
Look out for my two companions on your journey.

Welcome TO
Invisible Journeys

THE Highway

Travel along the Highway following
a message's journey from its source
(the brain) to its end (the people).

THE Byways

On your journey you will be asked
to select your own route. Choose
a Byway and follow the path.

THE Show Zones

The Byways lead you to Show Zones,
which contain vital information about
your trip. These may lead you further –
watch out for Zone Overload panels,
they are bursting with fascinating facts.
Visible Proof Spots will test your
knowledge with experiments and puzzles.
Bypass Buttons allow you to leap
forward to Show Zones further along
the route. They have a symbol that looks
like this. ------------------------------⟶
Let's begin our journey!

Bypass
BUTTON

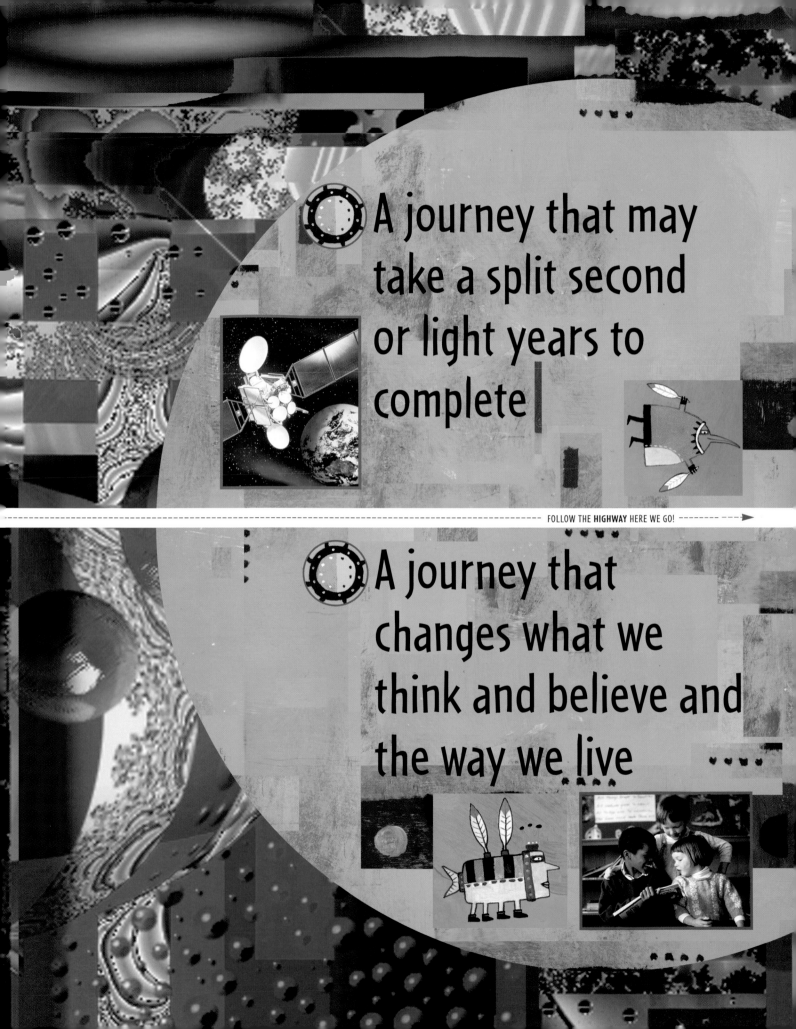

A journey that may take a split second or light years to complete

A journey that changes what we think and believe and the way we live

All communication begins in the

Brain

FOLLOW THE **HIGHWAY** - - - - - - - - - - - - - - - - - →

This is where our journey starts – right in the middle of the human brain.

Imagine!
Nerve impulses in the brain can travel at 290km/h – as fast as some racing cars!

The brain is the most complex body organ. Let's take a look at it.

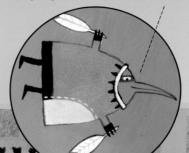

Select
YOUR BYWAY

The Brain

1 What is the brain?
(AND WHAT DOES IT DO?)
- - - - → BYWAY TO SHOW

2 What does the brain look like?
(HOW BIG IS IT AND WHAT WOULD IT FEEL LIKE TO TOUCH?)
- - - - → BYWAY TO SHOW

3 Where did the brain come from?
(DOES EVERY LIVING CREATURE HAVE A BRAIN?)
- - - - → BYWAY TO SHOW

4 How does the brain work?
(CAN THE BRAIN STOP WORKING PROPERLY?)
- - - - → BYWAY TO SHOW

1 What is the brain?

The brain is the most powerful and complicated organ in the human body. It is the body's control centre. The brain floats in a fluid inside the head and is protected by layers of skin, called meninges, and the thick bones of the skull, called the cranium. A network of blood vessels supplies the brain with oxygen.

Bypass BUTTON

DO ALL LIVING CREATURES HAVE BRAINS? FIND OUT IN SHOW ZONE 3.

Visible Proof SPOT

Stack a row of dominoes closely in front of each other. When you knock the first domino down, it causes the rest to topple, one by one. Signals are passed between neurons in a similar way. Electrical pulses are fired off one after another, down the axon until they reach the next neuron.

JUST WHY IS THE BRAIN SO IMPORTANT? FOLLOW THE PATH TO THE **ZONE OVERLOAD**.

What's inside the brain?

The brain is made up of billions of cells. There are two kinds of cells.

1 NERVE CELLS (CALLED NEURONS) The electrical and chemical signals that pass from one neuron to the next are responsible for everything we do, feel and think. The human brain has from 10 billion to 100 billion neurons, which are all connected. One tiny neuron is linked to thousands of others.

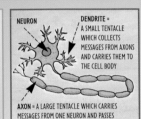

NEURON
DENDRITE = A SMALL TENTACLE WHICH COLLECTS MESSAGES FROM AXONS AND CARRIES THEM TO THE CELL BODY

AXON = A LARGE TENTACLE WHICH CARRIES MESSAGES FROM ONE NEURON AND PASSES THEM TO ANOTHER NEURON

2 SUPPORTING CELLS (CALLED NEUROGLIA, OR GLIA) Although the glia cannot send signals, they are very important because they protect the neurons and keep the brain free from disease.

FOLLOW THE **HIGHWAY** TO FIND OUT ABOUT THE MESSAGES WE SEND

ZONE Overload

This organ controls the human body.

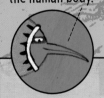

And what does the brain do?

The brain receives information about what is going on inside and outside the body. It then analyses this information and sends messages out to parts of the body, causing them to act in a certain way.

LOOKING AT BRAINWAVES

Even when you are asleep, the brain is still active, keeping the body alive. Doctors can use an electroencephalograph (EEG) to record the electrical activity, or brain waves, in a person's brain. The EEG patterns show what is happening when the person is awake or asleep.

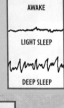

AWAKE

LIGHT SLEEP

DEEP SLEEP

Bypass BUTTON

TO FIND OUT EXACTLY HOW THE BRAIN DOES ALL THIS, TURN TO **SHOW ZONE** 4.

1 The brain controls our behaviour.

2 The brain allows us to move.

3 The brain makes all the different parts of the body work.

4 The brain stores information from our past, helping us to learn and remember.

5 The brain allows us to think and feel.

6 The brain lets us use language to communicate.

HOW BIG IS THE BRAIN? FOLLOW THE **BYWAY** TO SHOW ZONE 2

WHERE DID THE BRAIN COME FROM? FOLLOW THE **BYWAY** TO SHOW ZONE 3

WHAT MAKES THE BRAIN WORK? FOLLOW THE **BYWAY** TO SHOW ZONE 4

2

What does the brain look like?

The human brain is like a ball of jelly, with grooves and ridges covering its surface. It is greyish pink in colour.

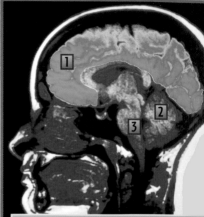

THE THREE PARTS OF THE BRAIN

1 THE CEREBRUM This is made up of neurons and glia.

※ It is the largest part of the brain, making up more than three-quarters of the total weight. It has many folds and grooves.

※ A fissure (a large groove) divides the cerebrum into halves, called the left cerebral hemisphere and the right cerebral hemisphere. The outer layer of the cerebrum is called the cortex.

※ Each hemisphere is divided into four regions, called lobes.

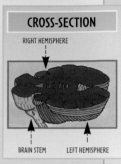

CROSS-SECTION

RIGHT HEMISPHERE

BRAIN STEM   LEFT HEMISPHERE

1 Responsible for intelligence and feelings.

2 Controls balance, posture and movement.

3 Looks after the processes of the body, such as brea

FOLLOW THE **HIGHWAY** AND FIND OUT ABOUT THOUGHT AND IMAGINATION

3

Where did the brain come from

The first living animals were invertebrates – animals without backbones. Invertebrates do not have well-developed brains. Instead, their bodies are controlled by clusters of nerve cells, called ganglia. Scientists believe that the human brain developed gradually, or evolved, from ganglia.

THE GROWTH OF THE BRAIN BEFORE A CHILD IS BORN

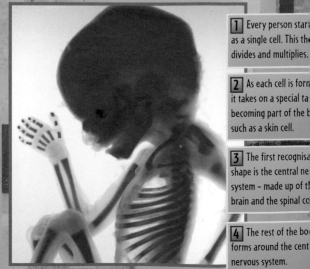

1 Every person star as a single cell. This th divides and multiplies.

2 As each cell is forr it takes on a special ta becoming part of the b such as a skin cell.

3 The first recognisa shape is the central ne system – made up of t brain and the spinal co

4 The rest of the bo forms around the cent nervous system.

BYWAY TO SHOW ZONE 2

WHAT ARE THE THREE PARTS OF THE BRAIN? FOLLOW THE **BYWAY** TO SHOW ZONE 2

BYWAY TO SHOW ZONE 3

BYWAY TO SHOW ZONE 4

THE CEREBELLUM

...is made up of closely-linked bundles of nerve cells, ...ed folia. It has a right and a ... hemisphere which link the ...erent sides of the cerebrum ...he rest of the body.

THE BRAIN STEM

...s is like a long stalk. It ...nects the cerebrum with ... spinal cord. The bottom ...t of the brain stem, or ...dulla, controls the body's ...al processes, such as the ...rtbeat and breathing.

...OW THE PATH TO THE **ZONE OVERLOAD** ...ND OUT ABOUT THE BRAIN'S SIZE.

ZONE

Overload
Is the brain always the same size?

How big is the brain?

The average weight of an adult human brain is around 1.4kg.

COMPARING BRAIN SIZES

NEWBORN BABY = BRAIN WEIGHS 0.5KG

SIX-YEAR-OLD = BRAIN AT ITS FULL WEIGHT OF 1.4KG

The brain becomes heavier because the neurons grow in size as you grow. The number of connections between the neurons also increases – axons grow new branches, which link up with the tentacle-like dendrites. The greater the number of connections, the more complex your thinking can be.

AND WHAT WOULD IT FEEL LIKE TO TOUCH?

SMOOTH AND SPRINGY, LIKE A HARD JELLY!

Bypass
BUTTON

TO FIND OUT MORE ABOUT THE DIFFERENCES BETWEEN THE RIGHT AND LEFT HEMISPHERES, GO TO **SHOW ZONE 4**.

Visible Proof **SPOT**

Clench both of your hands into fists and put them together. That's about the size of your brain!

Bypass
BUTTON

FIND OUT MORE ABOUT THOUGHT IN **SHOW ZONE 6**.

------------------ FOLLOW THE **HIGHWAY** ------>

ZONE

Overload
Are all animal brains the same?

Does every living creature have a brain?

THE BRAIN AT BIRTH

...wborn baby's brain has up to 100 ...n neurons. At the start, most of the ...ons are not connected. But as the ...grows older and learns and gains ...experiences, connections are made ...d broken – between the cells, and ...rain develops and grows. When ...ons die, they are not replaced.

...irth, neurons are ...spaced.

※ As learning takes place, neurons form links.

...OW THE PATH TO THE ZONE **OVERLOAD** TO ...VER IF EVERY ANIMAL HAS A BRAIN.

Simple animals, such as worms and insects, have brains made up of just a few groups of nerve cells. Animals with backbones (vertebrates) have complicated brains.

1. Sharks and fish have simple brains.

2. Birds and reptiles have a larger cerebrum.

3. Mammals have the most well-developed brains.

Bypass
BUTTON

FIND OUT HOW THE SIZE OF THE BRAIN AFFECTS HOW CLEVER A CREATURE IS IN **SHOW ZONE 7**.

MADE TO MEASURE

In some animals, parts of the brain may be particularly developed to give them special skills that help them to survive.

※ Birds and fish that migrate are able to navigate their way across vast distances.

※ A dog's sense of smell may be a million times more acute than a human's.

CAN THE BRAIN GO WRONG? **BYWAY** TO SHOW ZONE 4 --->

4

How does the brain work?

All our actions, thoughts and ideas are controlled by the brain. The billions of neurons in the brain pass messages, in the form of electrical impulses, between them, and then around the body through the nervous system.

Different areas of the brain receive information from our sense organs, such as the eyes and ears. The brain acts on this information by sending messages to the relevant parts of the body, such as the muscles and organs.

WHAT HAPPENS WHEN THE BRAIN GOES WRONG? FOLLOW THE PATH TO THE **ZONE OVERLOAD**.

SENDING A MESSAGE FROM ONE NEURON TO ANOTHER

1 The message is carried away from the cell body of the neuron along the axon. Messages can travel along nerves at speeds of up to 90 metres per second!

2 Neurons do not quite touch one another. When the message reaches the end of the axon, it has to cross a tiny gap – called a synapse – between the axon and a dendrite of the next cell.

3 Electrical impulses cannot cross the synapse – but chemical impulses can. So the message triggers knobs on the end of the axon into releasing a special chemical, called a neurotransmitter. The neurotransmitter bridges the synaptic gap.

4 When enough neurotransmitter has built up at the dendrite, it fires an electrical impulse of its own and the message continues its journey.

RESPONDING T THE SIGNAL

Each part of the brai responsible for diffe actions. These variou control centres deco the message and the instruct the body on what to do.

☐ HEARING	☐ SME
■ TALKING	☐ MOV
☐ SEEING	☐ TOU
■ UNDERSTANDING	■ THIN

FOLLOW THE **HIGHWAY** AND FIND OUT WHAT MAKES US THINK

ZONE

Overload

What makes the brain not work properly?

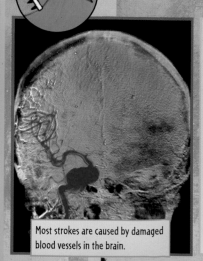

Most strokes are caused by damaged blood vessels in the brain.

Can the brain stop working properly?

Accidents and disease may damage the brain. Some people are born with brain disorders. If part of the brain is not working it may cause mental illness or physical disability.

※ If the supply of blood to the brain is cut off, neurons in that area will die. The part of the body controlled by the neurons may stop working. This is called a stroke. It mainly affects old people, causing speech difficulties or parts of the body to become paralysed. Effects are often temporary.
※ Parkinson's disease also mainly occurs in old age. It destroys the neurons that make dopamine, a chemical used by the brain to control movement. The common symptoms of stiff muscles and trembling limbs may be treated by drugs.

 Visible Proof SPOT

Our brain stores pictures in its memo The brain will recognise a picture even if you only see a small part of it, or if you see a hazy outline. Who is this famous person?

ANSWER: MICHAEL JACKSON.

THE RIGHT AND LEFT HEMISPHERES

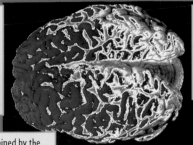

LEFT CEREBRAL HEMISPHERE controls [the] right-hand side of [the] body. It is used for [speech], language and [functions] that need [order] and logic.

THE RIGHT CEREBRAL HEMISPHERE controls the left-hand side of the body. It is used for creative thinking and imagination.

[The] hemispheres are joined by the [COR]PUS CALLOSUM, which allows us [to use] both hemispheres at the same [time]. This means, for example, that [we] can read a word and visualise the [obje]ct at the same time.

Bypass
BUTTON

FIND OUT MORE ABOUT IMAGINATION IN **SHOW ZONE 9**.

Visible Proof SPOT

To use the left-hand side of your brain, work out which number comes next: 3, 3, 5, 4, 4, 3, 5, 5, 4, ? To use the right-hand side of your brain, play a musical instrument or draw a picture!

ANSWER: 3 – THE NUMBER OF LETTERS IN THE WORDS 'ONE', 'TWO', 'THREE', ETC.

FINDING OUT MORE

There are many areas of the human mind that people do not understand. Scientists study the brain to try to find out more. Neurologists study neurons and the nervous system.

※ **CRANIOLOGISTS** study the shape and size of the skull.

※ **PSYCHOLOGISTS** study people's behaviour.

※ **PSYCHIATRISTS** study brain illnesses and disorders.

KEEPING THE BRAIN ALIVE

※ The brain needs a constant supply of oxygen to keep it working.

※ The brain needs energy from food. When the body has broken down the food into glucose, the glucose passes through the bloodstream to the brain.

※ A fifth of the body's blood and oxygen supplies are needed for the brain – yet the brain takes up just 2% of the body's total weight.

In his book *The Man who Mistook his Wife for a Hat*, the American doctor Oliver Sacks (right) wrote of many rare cases of brain disorder. One man found that when he looked at faces, he could only make out separate features. He could not put the features together to recognise who the person was – not even his own wife! The part of his brain which controlled visual information contained damaged neurons.

Let's examine how we go about making a message.

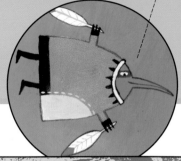

Select
YOUR BYWAY

Messages

5 What is communication? (WHY IS IT IMPORTANT?) ·········· → **BYWAY** TO SHOW ZONE 5

6 What is thought? ·········· → **BYWAY** TO SHOW ZONE 6

7 Are some people more intelligent than others? ·········· → **BYWAY** TO SHOW ZONE 7

8 How do we learn to communicate? (HOW DO WE REMEMBER?) ·········· → **BYWAY** TO SHOW ZONE 8

9 What is imagination? ·········· → **BYWAY** TO SHOW ZONE 9

Creative!
Some people use their imagination to describe the world in a new way.

9

5 What is communication?

Communication is the sharing of information, ideas and thoughts with others.

ONE TO ONE

Individuals communicate their desires, emotions and opinions to one another. This is called **PERSONAL COMMUNICATION**.

We talk to each other.
We use facial expressions.
We use our bodies.
We write, draw or create something.

COMMUNICATING TO THE MASSES

People may want to share information with many people. This is called **MASS COMMUNICATION**.

PEOPLE MAY USE:
books
newspapers
radio
television
computers

Bypass BUTTON

FIND OUT MORE ABOUT THE SPOKEN WORD IN **SHOW ZONE 11**.

Bypass BUTTON

SOME EVENTS REVOLUTIONISED TH_ WAY MASS COMMUNICAT_ COULD TAKE PLACE. SEE **SHOW ZONE 13**.

Visible Proof SPOT

How many kinds of communication are taking place in this picture?

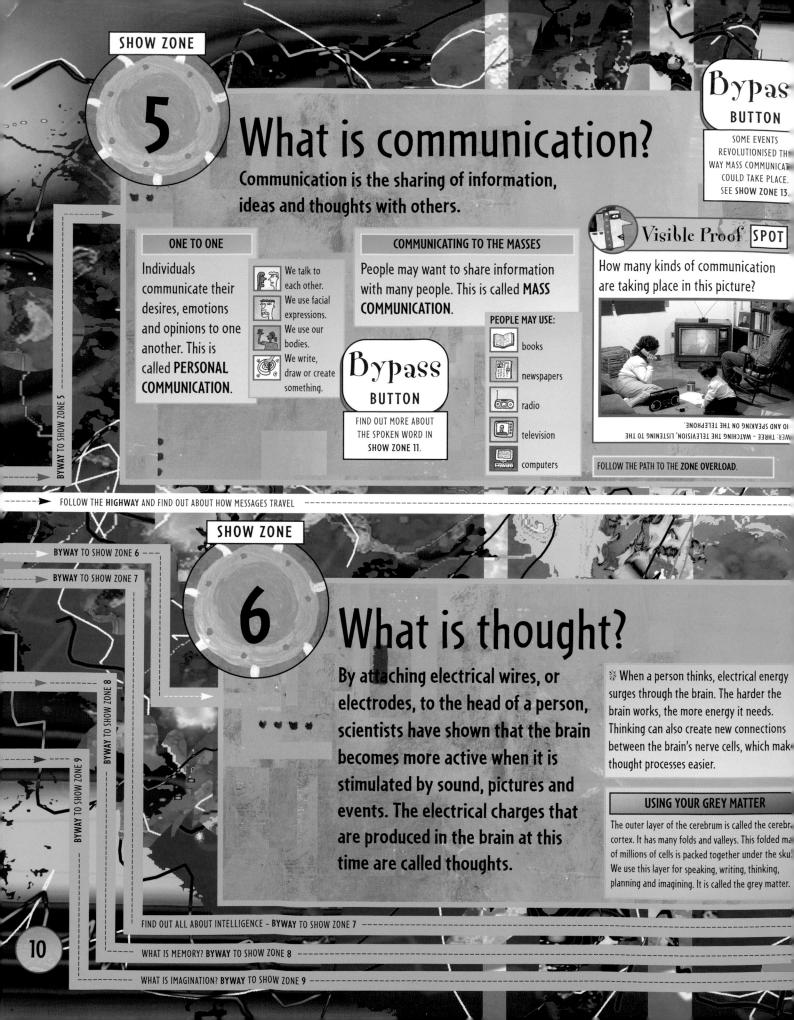

_WER: THREE – WATCHING THE TELEVISION, LISTENING TO THE _IO AND SPEAKING ON THE TELEPHONE.

FOLLOW THE PATH TO THE **ZONE OVERLOAD**.

FOLLOW THE **HIGHWAY** AND FIND OUT ABOUT HOW MESSAGES TRAVEL

BYWAY TO SHOW ZONE 5
BYWAY TO SHOW ZONE 6
BYWAY TO SHOW ZONE 7
BYWAY TO SHOW ZONE 8
BYWAY TO SHOW ZONE 9

6 What is thought?

By attaching electrical wires, or electrodes, to the head of a person, scientists have shown that the brain becomes more active when it is stimulated by sound, pictures and events. The electrical charges that are produced in the brain at this time are called thoughts.

※ When a person thinks, electrical energy surges through the brain. The harder the brain works, the more energy it needs. Thinking can also create new connections between the brain's nerve cells, which mak_ thought processes easier.

USING YOUR GREY MATTER

The outer layer of the cerebrum is called the cerebr_ cortex. It has many folds and valleys. This folded ma_ of millions of cells is packed together under the sku_ We use this layer for speaking, writing, thinking, planning and imagining. It is called the grey matter.

FIND OUT ALL ABOUT INTELLIGENCE – **BYWAY** TO SHOW ZONE 7

WHAT IS MEMORY? **BYWAY** TO SHOW ZONE 8

WHAT IS IMAGINATION? **BYWAY** TO SHOW ZONE 9

Why is communication important?

We all have feelings and a desire to express the way we feel. Most people are naturally curious. They want to know what is going on in the world around them. By sharing our knowledge and experiences with each other we learn more about people and about ourselves. Communication lets humans progress and change, or evolve.

Visible Proof SPOT

The message people choose to communicate often depends on their viewpoint. Examine the front pages of two different newspapers reporting the same event. How does each paper present the story? Does it have a certain slant, or bias? What about the headline, or the opening paragraph? What is each paper trying to tell its readers?

Bypass
BUTTON
HAVE COMMUNICATION ADVANCES MADE THE WORLD A BETTER PLACE? SEE **SHOW ZONE 22**.

FOLLOW THE **HIGHWAY**

SHOW ZONE

7

Are some people more intelligent than others?

Bypass
BUTTON
SOME OF THE MOST INTELLIGENT PEOPLE HAVE SENT MESSAGES THAT HAVE SHAKEN THE WORLD. SEE **SHOW ZONE 21**.

TEST THE BRAIN
Some people believe that an intelligence test measures how clever someone is. A person has to solve problems involving memory, logic, sequences and calculations. Their score is used to calculate a number known as their intelligence quotient (IQ).

There is no link between the size of a person's brain and how clever that person is. Intelligence depends on many things, including the physical nature of the brain, the number and types of connections between the nerve cells, and how a person has been trained to use the brain.

GENE POWER
Every cell in your body contains thousands of instructions, called genes. Genes control characteristics such as your eye colour, nose shape and hair thickness and are passed down through families. Genes are also partly responsible for intelligence.

ENVIRONMENT POWER
What happens to you during your life also determines how clever you are. If information is scarce or you are not encouraged to learn, you may not develop your intelligence to its full power. So stimulate your brain by reading, discussing and problem-solving!

BYWAY TO SHOW ZONE 8
BYWAY TO SHOW ZONE 9

8

How do we learn to communicate?

Visible Proof SPOT
We learn to communicate by seeing how people around us interact with each other. Do you have an accent - a particular way of speaking? Do you use special words and phrases that only you and your friends understand?

Children learn from an early age to imitate the sounds they hear around them. They also learn to discard those sounds which they are capable of making, but which are not used by others.

Bypass BUTTON
FIND OUT MORE ABOUT THE SPOKEN WORD IN **SHOW ZONE 11.**

FOLLOW THE PATH TO THE **ZONE OVERLOAD.**

LEARNING TO GET THE MESSAGE ACROSS

2-3 MONTHS: Babies smile and make speech-like sound.

6 MONTHS: Babies start to develop unique personalities. They choose to do things, such as holding their bottles, in their own way.

12-18 MONTHS: Babies start to imitate older people. They say their first words.

18 MONTHS: A child knows 10-20 words and starts to join them together to make phrases.

3 YEARS: A child will have learnt about 900 words.

- - - -> FOLLOW THE **HIGHWAY** AND FIND OUT HOW WE SEND MESSAGES - - - - - - - - - -

ZONE
Overload
What is memory?

How do we remember?

Memories are thought to be formed, and stored, in an area of the brain called the hippocampus. A memory is formed by repeatedly stimulating the same set of nerve cells, which makes the connections between the cells stronger. If we stop recalling an event, the neurons begin to lose their connections and the memory fades.

EACH PERSON HAS A LONG-TERM AND A SHORT-TERM MEMORY

❄ LONG-TERM MEMORY
This memory stores all the information we need to know to carry out our daily tasks. Examples include reading, writing and remembering who we are, what we do and where we live.

❄ SHORT-TERM MEMORY
Information stays in short-term memory for a few minutes up to a few hours. The information is either discarded or, if recalled often enough, transferred to the long-term memory.

PHOTOGRAPHIC MEMORIES
Some people have photographic, or eidetic, memories. They can glance at a scene or object and remember every detail. The French emperor Napoleon Bonaparte (1769-1821) could glance at a map and then recall every town and river on it.

Visible Proof SPOT
Play this game to test your friends' memories. Place 20 small objects on a tray - ask your friends to look at the objects for one minute, then cover them up with a cloth. How many items can each person remember?

9

What is imagination?

Imagination is the first stage of creativity. Many people use their imagination to leave the real world behind and create something new. Or they look at old ideas and put them together in a new way.

Bypass
BUTTON

WHICH OTHER SCIENTISTS HAVE USED THEIR IMAGINATION TO MAKE THEORIES THAT EXPLAIN THE WORLD? FIND OUT IN SHOW ZONE 21.

CREATIVE THOUGHTS COME FROM THE RIGHT-HAND SIDE OF THE BRAIN.

IMAGINATIVE MESSAGES TO THE WORLD

1 Daydreaming and make-believe can lead to important inventions and discoveries.

ALBERT EINSTEIN (1879-1955)
He put together his famous theory of relativity after daydreaming under a tree and imagining the path of a sunbeam!

2 Artists and writers use their imaginations to show the world in a new way.

VINCENT VAN GOGH (1853-1890)
This Dutch artist created powerful and lively paintings, which showed the loneliness and sadness he felt. He suffered a brain disorder that made him violent and depressed. Painting was his way of communicating his feelings to the world.

H G WELLS (1866-1946)
This English writer created science-fiction stories in which he imagined how the world might be in the future, or how the world could be different today. He wrote about people being invisible, or being able to travel through time in time machines.

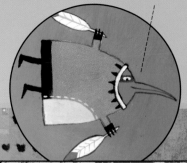

How does the message travel?

Select
YOUR BYWAY

The Message Travels

10 How were the first messages sent?

BYWAY TO SHOW ZONE 10

11 How do we get our message across today?

BYWAY TO SHOW ZONE 11

12 How and when do we send messages?
(WHAT OTHER FORMS OF COMMUNICATION HAVE BEEN USED?)

BYWAY TO SHOW ZONE 12

13 What important events revolutionised the way messages were sent?

BYWAY TO SHOW ZONE 13

14 How long does it take to send a message?
(AND HOW IS IT GETTING QUICKER AND EASIER TO SEND MESSAGES?)

BYWAY TO SHOW ZONE 14

15 How does the speed at which messages are made affect how long they will last?

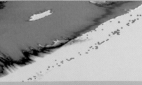

BYWAY TO SHOW ZONE 15

SHOW ZONE

10

How were the first messages se[nt]

Nobody knows for sure, but experts believe that prehistoric people probably passed information to each other using grunts and gestures. They may also have imitated the sounds of nature around them, such as the wind rushing through leaves or the cries of animals.

Bypass BUTTON

WHAT ARE SOME OF THE MOST FAMOUS MESSAGES OF ALL TIME? FIND OUT IN SHOW ZONE 20.

USING PICTURES (20,000 BC)

Pictures that represented animals, objects and events were used to tell stories.

This African cave painting shows a procession of people wearing bushy head-dresses.

BYWAY TO SHOW ZONE 10

BYWAY TO SHOW ZONE 11

FOLLOW THE **HIGHWAY** AND FIND OUT ABOUT WHAT HAPPENS WHEN A MESSAGE ARRIVES AT ITS DESTINATION

BYWAY TO SHOW ZONE 12

BYWAY TO SHOW ZONE 13

BYWAY TO SHOW ZONE 14

BYWAY TO SHOW ZONE 15

SHOW ZONE

11

How do we get our message across today?

There are many methods that we can use to relay our message to others, including words, pictures, codes and even our bodies.

WE USE LANGUAGE

The word language comes from the Latin 'lingua', meaning tongue. Most languages have both a writt[en] and a verbal form. There are about 6,000 languag[es] spoken around the world – and thousands more dialects, which are local variations on a language.

DIFFERENT COUNTRIES HAVE DIFFERENT WAYS TO SEND MESSAGES – **BYWAY** TO SHOW ZONE 12

INVENTIONS AND EVENTS HAVE CHANGED THE WAY WE SEND MESSAGES – **BYWAY** TO SHOW ZONE 13

SOME MESSAGES TAKE A LONG TIME GETTING FROM SENDER TO RECEIVER – **BYWAY** TO SHOW ZONE 14

SOME MESSAGES ARE BEAUTIFUL TO LOOK AT – **BYWAY** TO SHOW ZONE 15

THERE IS EVIDENCE OF OTHER EARLY FORMS OF WRITING: CHINESE (1500 BC), GREEK (1400 BC) AND LATIN (500 BC).

Visible Proof SPOT

Cuneiform symbols began as pictures drawn on their sides. Look at these original symbols. Can you guess what they represented?

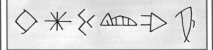

ANSWERS (L-R): THE SUN, GOD OR HEAVEN, MOUNTAIN, MAN, OX, FISH.

Gradually, the symbols were simplified into short, wedge-shaped strokes:

USING PICTURES TO REPRESENT WORDS (3500 BC)

The earliest known form of writing that could convey more complicated messages was developed by the Sumerians in the Middle East. It is called cuneiform writing. People drew pictures on clay tablets when they were soft. The clay was then left out in the sun until it hardened.

HIEROGLYPHS (3000 BC)

The ancient Egyptians sent messages using picture-like signs, called hieroglyphs, to represent words. The word hieroglyph means 'sacred carving'.

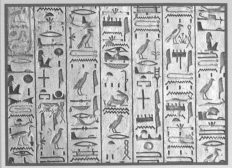

FOLLOW THE **HIGHWAY** ---▶

THE SPOKEN WORD We use conversation – when speaking face-to-face or by telephone. Some languages are only spoken by a few thousand people, are spoken by hundreds of millions.

The most widely spoken languages in the world are:
Mandarin Chinese = 825 million
English = 431 million
Hindi = 325 million
Spanish = 320 million
Russian = 187 million
Bengali = 178 million
Japanese = 124 million

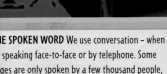

People use their hands to communicate with other. This is called sign language. There are for many different words and there is also a language alphabet.

2 THE WRITTEN WORD Rather than using pictures to represent objects, symbols were created to represent sounds. An early alphabet was developed by the Phoenicians around 1000 BC. We still use some of their characters in the Roman alphabet we use today.

PHOENICIAN	MODERN

A blind Frenchman called Louis Braille (1809-1852) was only 15 years old when he started to improve the system of writing for the blind. In his Braille alphabet, each letter is represented by a raised pattern of dots which are read with the fingertips.

Not everyone has the opportunity to read and write. In the USA, more than 97% of people can read and write, compared to 18% in Burkina Faso, West Africa.

WE USE CODES Codes help us to communicate in situations when we cannot speak or write to each other.

1 MORSE CODE Before the invention of the telephone, the quickest way of sending long-distance messages was by telegraph. Messages travelled along wires as electric signals. An American, Samuel Morse (1791-1872), developed one of the first electric telegraphs and used a code of dots and dashes.

2 SEMAPHORE

If ships at sea do not have radio contact, they may use a code called semaphore. Invented in 1860, sentences are spelt out by holding up two flags in particular positions to represent each letter of the alphabet.

WE USE OUR BODIES People use their faces and bodies to convey messages. This is called body language. The human face has 30 muscles which can be used to create different expressions.

BYWAY TO SHOW ZONE 12 ----▶

BYWAY TO SHOW ZONE 13 ----▶

BYWAY TO SHOW ZONE 14 ----▶

BYWAY TO SHOW ZONE 15 ----▶

15

12 How and when do we send messages?

How you send a message depends on the technology available to the sender of the message and the receiver, on circumstance and on the impact you want to make.

Bypa
BUTTON
LEAP TO SHOW ZO
TO FIND OUT MORE
COMMUNICATING
COMPUTER.

SOME PEOPLE HAVE MORE CHOICES THAN OTHERS – BYWAY TO SHOW ZONE 12

1 Using what is available

Throughout the world, people have access to different machines and tools. Some can choose from many communication methods; others have a more limited choice.

So, if you have something to tell someone, what do you do? Here are some choices.

POST

The first post, or pillar, boxes were erected in Britain in 1853. Before the introduction of stamps, the cost of posting a letter was paid by the person receiving it.

TELEPHONE

Alexander Graham Bell (1847-1922), right, a Scotsman who settled in the USA, invented the telephone in 1876. Telephones work by changing the voice's sound waves into an electric current, transmitting it down a network of wires and then changing it back into sound waves.

FOLLOW THE HIGHWAY AND FIND OUT HOW THE WAY WE COMMUNICATE HAS AFFECTED OUR LANDSCAPE

2 A question of circumstance

Not everybody has the same choices. Some groups of people live in small, and sometimes isolated, communities and have developed their own unique methods of communication.

3 Making an impact

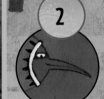

ADVERTISEMENTS

These are messages that are specially designed to sell or promote a product or an idea. Advertising is used by individuals, groups and governments to communicate ideas about themselves to other people. The content and look of an advertisement will depend on the kind of image the advertiser wants to reflect.

Visible Proof SPOT

What is this advertisement trying to tell you about the product being sold? Do you believe the message?

ANSWER: DRINKING THE PRODUCT WILL MAKE YOUR LIFE MUCH HAPPIER.

BYWAY TO SHOW ZONE 12

CERTAIN EVENTS HAVE CHANGED THE WAY WE COMMUNICATE – BYWAY TO SHOW ZONE 13

HOW HAS THE TIME NEEDED TO SEND A MESSAGE BEEN REDUCED? BYWAY TO SHOW ZONE 14

SOME MESSAGES ARE SENT IN A SIMPLE FORM, OTHERS ARE MORE ELABORATE – BYWAY TO SHOW ZONE 15

E-MAIL

first personal computer ... was the Altair, produced ... e USA in 1975. Today, PCs ... w users to send messages ... ach other on the screen ... econds, via electronic ..., or e-mail.

MOBILE TELEPHONE

Mobile, or cellular, telephones first appeared in Sweden in the late 1970s. Having no cords or cables, mobile phones can be used almost anywhere.

FAX

short for ...mile) is ...y of ...smitting, ...receiving, ...and ...es over telephone lines. ...e 1930s, newspapers first ...n using fax machines to ...smit photographs.

RADIO

In 1895, the Italian inventor Guglielmo Marconi (1874-1937) became the first person to send radio communication signals through the air. Today, there are about 25,000 radio stations in the world and two billion radio sets.

TELEVISION

Scottish engineer John Logie Baird (1888-1946) gave the first public demonstration of television in London in 1926. TV cameras work by changing pictures into electronic signals, which are then transmitted to the screen using radio waves.

ZONE Overload Some strange ways of sending messages!

What other forms of communication have been used?

Throughout history, people have sent messages in all kinds of unusual ways.

WALLS THAT SPELL WORDS

The ancient Greeks used a form of communication which involved lighting fires at various points along the tops of walls. Each part of the wall stood for a different letter of the alphabet – the receiver spelt out words according to where the fires were lit.

- - - - - FOLLOW THE **HIGHWAY** - - - - - - - >

MAPS MADE OF STICKS

More than 500 years ago, stick maps were used by people in some coastal regions to tell each other where nearby islands were and what the sea currents were like. Small shells marked the islands, while the currents were shown by the curves of the sticks.

MESSAGES IN THE MIND

Extrasensory perception (ESP) is communicating without using the five known senses. Some people claim to be able to receive messages, in the form of thoughts, directly from the minds of others. Most people doubt ESP exists because there is little scientific proof.

FIRST ADVERTISEMENTS

...00 BC Historians believe that the ...lonians, who lived in what is now ... were the first to use advertising. ... hung signs above their shop doors ... omote what they were selling. ...ols were used to represent the ...s for sale.

...00 BC In Egypt, merchants paid ...s to announce to passers-by that ...argo ships had arrived.

ART

Art is also a way of communicating ideas. Some artists have tried to express themselves and their ideas by using shapes and colour in innovative ways.

Surrealism was an art movement which began in Paris in 1924. Surrealist artists were interested in the mind and dreams. The Spanish painter Joan Miró (1893-1983) used round, curled and geometric symbols, and bright colours (above). His paintings were full of hidden messages.

FOLLOW THE PATH TO THE **ZONE OVERLOAD**.

Bypass
BUTTON
LEAP TO **SHOW ZONE 13** TO SEE WHICH INVENTIONS ALLOWED PEOPLE TO SEND THEIR MESSAGES MORE QUICKLY.

Bypass
BUTTON
WHAT WILL THE NEXT ADVANCES IN COMMUNICATION BE? LEAP TO **SHOW ZONE 23**.

13

What important events revolutionised the way messages were sent?

Some inventions and episodes in history opened up new ways of communicating for millions of people. These include the invention of paper and printing machines, the development of the postal system and the use of satellites and computers.

Bypass BUTTON

LEAP TO **SHOW ZONE 21** TO SEE HOW BOOKS HAVE BEEN USED TO SPREAD IDEAS AND BELIEFS.

WHAT PAPER IS LIKE DEPENDS O
※ The kind of pulp used - wood, cotton, linen, and so on.
※ The way the pulp is processed.
※ The type of machine used to ma the sheets of paper.

FOLLOW THE **HIGHWAY** TO FIND OUT HOW NEW COMMUNICATION METHODS HAVE AFFECTED WHERE PEOPLE LIVE AND WORK

FIND OUT ABOUT INVENTIONS AND EPISODES THAT CHANGED THE WORLD – **BYWAY** TO SHOW ZONE 13

3

The story of the Post

RELAY TEAMS

※ The first postal systems used either runners, or couriers on horseback. They were stationed at intervals along roads and passed messages on to each other. A string of couriers could carry messages more than 150km each day.

※ The Roman emperor Augustus Caesar built posthouses along the roads. These were resting places for messengers and their horses.

THE POST

※ In the 15th century, as the number of people who could read and write grew, more people started to communicate by letter. In Vienna, Austria, the Taxis family employed around 20,000 private couriers who worked across central Europe.

※ In the 17th century, governments across Europe started to set up public postal systems.

※ In 1837, a retired British teacher called Rowland Hill suggested a standard postage cost, regardless of the distance. Until then, the cost of posting a letter depended on how far it had to travel. He also proposed that the sender bought small labels - stamps - to stick on the letter so that the postage was paid for in advance.

MAIL ON THE RAIL

In the late 1880s, as the train networks developed, the postal system started to use special railway carriages which picked up post bags en route. Postal workers sorted the mail on-board as the train moved along.

※ **1789** The Unite States had 75 post offices.
※ **1901** This had increased to 77,000 post office
※ **1997** There are around 40,000 po offices. Although more messages ar sent, people have found other ways of communicating

Bypass BUTTON

LEAP TO **SHOW ZONE 15** TO FIND OUT WHICH ELECTRONIC DEVELOPMEN IS NOW AN ALTERNATIVE T TRADITIONAL MAIL.

The invention of paper

EGYPTIAN PAPYRUS

[In] ancient Egypt, papyrus reeds were cut into strips which were then [w]aved together and pressed into sheets. This textured material was [the] earliest form of paper, and was used for important documents.

CHINESE PULP

[Pa]per as we know it was invented by the Chinese more than 2,000 [ye]ars ago. It was made by pounding rope, rags or bark into a pulp [an]d then rolling it into sheets.

MACHINE-MADE PAPER

[Un]til the end of the 18th century, almost all paper was made by [h]and, sheet by sheet. In 1798, a Frenchman, Nicholas Louis Robert, [cr]eated a machine that could produce paper in long rolls.

The importance of printing machines

1 BLOCK PRINTING The first form of printing was made by the Chinese around AD 100. First, they carved pictures and letters on to wooden blocks. Then, they put ink on these designs and pressed paper on to the inked blocks, transferring the image on to the paper.

2 MOVABLE TYPE Around 1045, a Chinese printer, Bi Sheng, invented the first movable type. He made separate clay pieces for each character, or letter. These were then reused.

3 THE PRINTING PRESS
Around 1440, German metalsmith Johannes Gutenberg, developed the first printing press to use moveable type (right). It was adapted from a machine used to press grapes or cheese.

Visible Proof SPOT

How many printed items do you use everyday? What information do they give you? Examine this list and then make one of your own: books, comics, postcards, posters, advertisements.

HOW DID PRINTING CHANGE THE WORLD?
Printing allowed ideas, facts and knowledge to be passed to more people, more quickly and more cheaply than before. It encouraged people to learn how to read and write.

Bypass BUTTON

ARE SOME BOOKS SO BEAUTIFUL THAT THEY ARE CONSIDERED WORKS OF ART? LEAP TO **SHOW ZONE 15** TO FIND OUT.

FOLLOW THE **HIGHWAY** ⸻▶

Artificial satellites in space

An artificial satellite is any manufactured object that circles a planet. Communications satellites orbit the Earth and allow people to pass messages from one side of the world to the other, relatively quickly. The first artificial satellite, Sputnik 1, was launched by the Soviet Union in 1957. Today, there are more than 2,000 satellites orbiting the Earth.

HOW DO COMMUNICATIONS SATELLITES WORK?

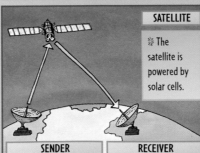

SATELLITE
※ The satellite is powered by solar cells.

SENDER
※ A telecommunications station has a dish-shaped aerial that points at the satellite. The aerial transmits radio signals to the satellite.

RECEIVER
※ The signals are beamed back from the satellite to an aerial in a telecommunications station in another part of the world.

※ Each communications satellite can relay television pictures and many telephone calls at the same time.

A chip that changed the world

The first silicon chip (also called an integrated circuit) was produced in 1958. A chip is the brain of an electronic machine. It may be no bigger than a fingernail, yet it contains all the information needed to make complicated machines, such as computers, cameras and mobile telephones, work.

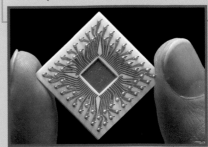

14

How long does it take to send a message?

That depends on how the message is being sent and where it is going from and to. In the past, messages took much longer to reach their destinations.

FOLLOW THE PATH TO THE ZONE OVERLOAD.

SENDING A MESSAGE FROM LONDON TO NEW YORK...		
DATE MESSAGE SENT	METHOD OF SENDING MESSAGE	TIME LAPSE BETWEEN SENDING AND RECEIVING
1750	SAILING SHIP	FROM 6 TO 9 WEEKS
1840	FAST SAILING SHIPS CALLED CLIPPERS	AROUND 12 DAYS
1858	FIRST TRANSATLANTIC TELEGRAPH	SECONDS
1956	FIRST TRANSATLANTIC TELEPHONE CALL	SECONDS
1958	FIRST COMMUNICATIONS SATELLITE	IMMEDIATE
1970	FIRST OVERSEAS DIRECT DIAL PHONE CALL	IMMEDIATE
1990s	COMPUTERS	POTENTIALLY IMMEDIATE

FOLLOW THE **HIGHWAY** TO FIND OUT WHAT IMPACT SOME MESSAGES HAVE HAD ON THE WORLD

WHAT WAS THE INDUSTRIAL REVOLUTION? BYWAY TO SHOW ZONE 14

ZONE Overload

Why timing can be crucial.

And how is it getting quicker and easier to send messages?

Human beings are constantly striving for technological advance. Scientists and inventors seek to improve the links between individuals or between larger groups of people.

HOW DO MOBILE PHONES WORK?

The area covered by a mobile telephone network is divided up into cells. Each cell has a relay station that can receive and transmit signals. When a person makes a call, the mobile phone transmits radio waves to the nearest relay station. This directs it either to a standard telephone network or to another mobile phone user.

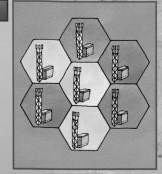

Portable satellite terminals are being developed for people working in isolated areas. These will fit into a pocket and will allow a person to send messages even if the area is not linked to a telecommunications network.

Bypas
BUTTON

CAN ADVANCES IN COMMUNICATION TECHNOLOGY HAVE NEGATIVE EFFECT? TO FIND OUT, LEAP T SHOW ZONE 22.

SOME PEOPLE HAVE LABOURED OVER THEIR MESSAGES – OTHERS PRODUCE SOMETHING MORE THROWAWAY – BYWAY TO SHOW ZONE 15

you are speaking on the telephone to
friend in another country, there may
e a short delay between your friend
peaking and you hearing their voice.
his time-delay
appens because
he radio signals
hat carry the sound
ometimes travel
ong distances up to
satellite and then
ack down again.

Bypass
BUTTON

WHAT EFFECT DID THE
INDUSTRIAL REVOLUTION
HAVE ON WHERE PEOPLE
LIVED? LEAP TO
SHOW ZONE 17.

THEN AND NOW...

❋ **Around 1200 BC**
When the Greeks
captured the city of
Troy, they lit bonfires
on hills to tell the
people in Argos,
800km away, that
they had won the
Trojan War. This was
the fastest way to spread the news.

❋ **1985** The 'Live Aid'
concerts in London and
Philadelphia were beamed
live across the world, by
12 satellites, and viewed
by about 1.6 billion
people. The concerts
raised money for starving
people in Africa.

A RUSH OF ACTIVITY AND NEW IDEAS

The late 19th century was a time when many new machines
were invented, and goods and materials became mass-
produced. This changed and usually improved the way people
communicated. In Britain, this time in history is known as the
Industrial Revolution.

1 TYPEWRITER
This machine was
invented in 1868 by
three Americans.
Writing by hand was
no longer the only
way to send a
written message.

2 PHONOGRAPH
The phonograph was
created in 1877 by
the American
inventor Thomas
Edison (1847-1931).
It recorded sound by
a needle vibrating
against a cylinder
wrapped in foil.

3 RADIO
In 1895, Guglielmo
Marconi sent the
first telegraph
signals through the
air rather than
along wires.

-------- FOLLOW THE **HIGHWAY** --------▶

WHAT IS THE INTERNET?

etwork is a set of computers that are linked
ether – people can pass information from one
mputer terminal to another. The Internet, or 'Net',
massive network made up of thousands of
aller computer networks, which are connected by
international telephone system.

WHO INVENTED THE INTERNET?
The Internet was created in the late
1960s, when the US army
joined together military and
government computers. This
complicated network was designed
so that if some of the computers
were destroyed in a war, messages
could still get through the
undamaged links. Soon, universities,
businesses and individuals were
allowed to add their computers to
the network. By the year 2000, an
estimated 750 million people will be
linked to the Internet.

THE IMPORTANCE OF GETTING THE RIGHT MESSAGE ACROSS

Getting the right message to the right person at the
right time may be crucial. The war of 1812 between
Britain and the United States should never have
happened. On 18 June, the US declared war on Britain
for troubling its ships. Britain had, in fact, decided to
stop interfering with US ships two days before. But by
the time the message had travelled across the Atlantic
Ocean by ship, the war had begun.

Bypass
BUTTON

WHAT IS ELECTRONIC MAIL?
LEAP TO **SHOW ZONE 15**
TO FIND OUT.

BYWAY TO SHOW ZONE 15 -------▶

15

How does the speed at which messages are made affect how long they will last?

Before the invention of the printing press, books had to be copied by hand by scribes. One book could take months to complete. Each copy was unique and thought to be precious.

We made it from the sender to the receiver – prepare for impact!

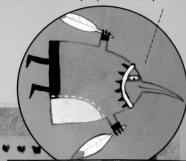

Arrival
AT DESTINATION
THE MESSAGE REACHES THE
People

FOLLOW THE **HIGHWAY** TO THE ARRIVAL ZONE

PRESERVING THE MESSAGE

During the Middle Ages (5th-16th centuries), monks in Europe developed great skills in writing and bookmaking. The manuscripts that they produced have been preserved and admired for hundreds of years. This is because their work was beautiful and rare.

The Book of Kells is an illuminated manuscript of the Gospels. Letters are highly decorated with gold and borders have brightly-coloured pictures and patterns. This book was produced in the eighth century at the monastery of Kells in County Meath, Ireland.

THROWAWAY MESSAGES

Today, networks link computers to each other. This allows users to 'post' electronic mail, or e-mail, from machine to machine. A message typed into the sender's computer passes along the network and is delivered into the receiver's computer. This can take just a few seconds, even if the sender and receiver are thousands of miles apart. Once the message has been received, it is generally discarded to keep the computer's memory free. Important messages may be saved onto a disk or printed out.

Bypass
BUTTON
WHAT CAN WE EXPECT TO HAPPEN TO IMPROVE COMMUNICATION IN THE FUTURE? LEAP TO SHOW ZONE 23.

WHO DECORATED THEIR MESSAGES WITH GOLD? BYWAY TO SHOW ZONE 15

Sending messages can have an impact on the landscape.

Select
YOUR BYWAY

Impact
ON PLANET EARTH

16 How does the way we communicate affect the environment we live in?

BYWAY TO SHOW ZONE 16

17 How has communication influenced what we build and where we build it?

BYWAY TO SHOW ZONE 17

FOLLOW THE **HIGHWAY**

16 How does the way we communicate affect the environment we live in?

Sometimes, in order for messages to travel and be received, certain technology must be in place. This may change the look of the surrounding landscape.

BYWAY TO SHOW ZONE 16

1 Cables

A cable is made up of an insulated bundle of metal wires or fibres. Cables are widely used to transmit communication signals, either in the form of electric currents or as pulses of light.

1 TELEPHONE CABLES

Following the invention of the telephone in 1876, telephone cables strung between tall poles became a common sight in towns and cities.

2 UNDERGROUND CABLES

One way of preventing the landscape from becoming cluttered is to bury cables underground. But even this causes disruption to the immediate countryside when the topsoil is dug up.

FOLLOW THE **HIGHWAY** TO FIND OUT HOW SOME MESSAGES HAVE CHANGED THE LIVES OF THE PEOPLE WHO RECEIVED THEM

17

BYWAY TO SHOW ZONE 17

3 Satellite dishes and aerials

※ A house or business may have an individual aerial, or satellite dish, attached to its wall or roof for receiving television signals.

The world's tallest free-standing structure is the CN Tower – a broadcasting tower in Toronto, Ontario, Canada, that rises to 553m.

※ Broadcasting aerials are built on tall towers, and usually on high ground, to help distribute the signals widely.

4 Advertising messages

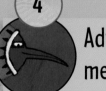

Advertisers, keen to attract the attention of potential customers, may resort to brash gimmicks. Huge hoardings, neon signs, flashing lights, video screens and eye-catching designs may overwhelm the surrounding environment.

IN BRITAIN

※ 1800s
80% of the population lived the country.
※ 1990s
90% of the population lives in cities.

Bypa
BUTTO

TODAY, COMMUN
TECHNOLOGY AL
TO LIVE AND WOR
SAME PLACE. LE
SHOW ZONE

24

Pylons

Electricity, which is used to operate computers, fax machines and other hi-tech communication devices, is often carried in cables strung between tall metal towers, called pylons. Pylons can dominate large stretches of the countryside. Today, more and more cables are being laid under the ground.

Bypass
BUTTON
THE ENVIRONMENT CAN ALSO MAKE PEOPLE FEEL ISOLATED. SEE **SHOW ZONE 22**.

Some messages have shaken the world, while others have changed it forever...

Select
YOUR BYWAY

Impact
ON THE WAY PEOPLE LIVE

ow has communication fluenced what we build nd where we build it?

roved communication meant t people could move away m their families and still keep ouch. Factories were built to oduce goods, and towns and ies were constructed as people t rural areas to look for work ew industries.

25

18

How does communication make the world seem smaller?

BYWAY TO SHOW ZONE 18

Telecommunications have helped to bridge the gap between continents. Telephones, televisions, satellites and computers allow us to communicate almost instantly with people around the world. They give us a greater knowledge about how others live and what they believe in, and make the world seem a much smaller place.

TV TALES

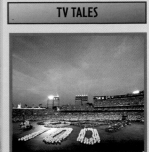

SATELLITE

TRANSMITTER

RECE

THE EVENT:
The 1996 Summer Olympic Games held at Atlanta, USA.

DISCOVER WHETHER OR NOT COMMUNICATION IS A GOOD THING! FOLLOW THE **HIGHWAY**

BYWAY TO SHOW ZONE 19

BYWAY TO SHOW ZONE 20

BYWAY TO SHOW ZONE 21

BYWAY TO SHOW ZONE 22

BYWAY TO SHOW ZONE 23

19

How has the way in which we communicate changed the world?

The advances in communication technology have influenced every aspect of our lives...

1

The way we live

❊ **TELEVISION** gives us news about the world.
❊ **EFFECTS** We may read less. We may travel less, learning about countries by watching TV programmes rather than by visiting the places.

❊ **TELEPHONES** help us to keep in touch.
❊ **EFFECTS** We may write fewer letters and travel less often to see people. We may lose some of our privacy.

SOME MESSAGES HAVE BEEN REMEMBERED THROUGHOUT HISTORY - BYWAY TO SHOW ZONE 20

SOME MESSAGES CHANGED THE WORLD FOREVER - BYWAY TO SHOW ZONE 21

IS IT TIME TO STOP ADVANCING COMMUNICATION TECHNOLOGY? BYWAY TO SHOW ZONE 22

WHAT CAN WE EXPECT TO HAPPEN NEXT? BYWAY TO SHOW ZONE 23

Bypass
BUTTON

...NG LEARNED TO SEND
...SSAGES AROUND THE
...LOBE, WE ARE NOW
...MING OUT MESSAGES TO
...ER GALAXIES! LEAP TO
...SHOW ZONE 23.

DIRECT CONTACT

✻ Being able to discuss subjects on screen with people you have never physically met also makes our planet seem a smaller place.

✻ The Internet has paved the way for a new kind of language. Users have developed a range of symbols, known as smileys or emoticons, that can be read and understood by most people from anywhere in the world.

Visible Proof SPOT

Match the smileys to their correct meanings.

1 User is laughing   A :-|
2 User is being serious   B |-O
3 User is yawning   C :-D

ANSWERS: 1=C; 2=A; 3=B.

NOT THE WHOLE PICTURE

Of course, we can only experience what is presented to us. In many cases, messages are cut, or edited, to fit into a time slot or organised to convey a particular programme-maker's viewpoint.

...UR EXPERIENCE:
...e Games were broadcast
... more than 170 countries
...d watched on TV by about
...o billion people each day.

Not everyone has access to the same technology. In developing countries, telecommunications may only be available to the rich minority; for the poorer majority, the world can still seem a big and bewildering place.

FOLLOW THE **HIGHWAY** ---▶

2

The way we work

Bypass
BUTTON

WHAT EFFECT COULD THIS KIND OF LIFESTYLE HAVE ON THE HUMAN RACE? LEAP TO **SHOW ZONE 22**.

✻ **COMPUTERS** allow workers
...n different buildings, cities and
...even countries to be linked.
✻ **EFFECTS** People work from
...home instead of from an office,
...communicating with each other
...via phones, fax machines and
...computer networks.

Sometimes tradition is more important than technological advances. An example of a communication method that has remained unchanged for centuries can be found in Islam, the Muslim religion. A muezzin calls followers to prayers five time a day. His distinctive, musical chant carries far and wide from his position high up in the tower, or minaret, attached to the mosque.

BYWAY TO SHOW ZONE 20 ----▶

BYWAY TO SHOW ZONE 21 ----▶

BYWAY TO SHOW ZONE 22 ----▶

BYWAY TO SHOW ZONE 23 ----▶

20 What are some of the most famous messages of all time?

We remember and preserve many communications because they convey important messages. Sometimes, the fact that a message has been sent and received is more important than its content. Other messages are remembered for their impact on the world.

MARATHON MAN (490 BC)

A messenger called Pheidippides ran the 40km distance from Marathon to Athens, Greece, to bring news of a Greek victory over the invading Persians. After delivering the message, he dropped to the floor, dead. His feat is commemorated by the marathon, a running race of about 42.2km.

MAYAN MESSAGES (1100-1500)

The Mayans, of central America, made fragile books from fig tree bark. They used elaborate pictures, or hieroglyphs, to record important dates, historical events and information about their gods. Only four of these books survived the Spanish invasion in the early 1500s. Experts are still trying to decode the mysterious symbols used in the Mayan texts.

FOLLOW THE **HIGHWAY** TO THE END OF YOUR JOURNEY

21 Which messages amazed the world?

Messages can amaze if they upset or surprise the people receiving them. Messages may also question, or overturn, commonly-held beliefs.

1 Religious messages

Many religions have collection of sacred writings:

CHRISTIANITY	BIBLE (left)
ISLAM	QURAN (above)
JUDAISM	TORAH
BUDDHISM	TRIPITAKA
HINDUISM	VEDAS
TAOISM	TAO TE CHING

HAS ALL THIS CHANGE MADE THE WORLD A BETTER PLACE? **BYWAY** TO SHOW ZONE 22

IMAGINING THE FUTURE - **BYWAY** TO SHOW ZONE 23

BYWAY TO SHOW ZONE 20

BYWAY TO SHOW ZONE 21

TITANIC TRAGEDY (1912)

The British passenger ship the *Titanic* was supposed to be unsinkable. But on the liner's first voyage, from Southampton, England, to New York, USA, it struck an iceberg and sank; 1,513 lives were lost. Newspapers around the world reacted to the disaster with a flurry of headlines, photographs, extended reports and special sections.

A MESSAGE FROM MARS (1938)

"Ladies and gentlemen, I have a grave announcement to make. Incredible as it may seem, strange beings who landed in New Jersey tonight are the vanguard of an invading army from Mars." Thousands of Americans panicked when they heard this radio message. But it was actually a play based on the H G Wells novel *The War of the Worlds*!

A SPEECH FROM SPACE (1969)

The American astronaut Neil Armstrong became the first person to set foot on the Moon. He spoke to the world, via satellite communication. This was his famous message: "That's one small step for a man, one giant leap for mankind."

FAMOUS FIRSTS

✻ **16 AUGUST 1858**
"Glory to God in the highest, on Earth peace, goodwill toward men." The first official communication sent over a transatlantic cable.

✻ **10 MARCH 1876**
"Mr Watson, come here. I want you!" The first telephone message – Alexander Graham Bell was calling for his assistant after accidentally spilling a jar of acid.

✻ **1927**
"Wait a minute, wait a minute. You ain't heard nothin' yet." Al Jolson, in the first talking film, *The Jazz Singer*.

BURNING BEACONS (1588)

...n people lit ...ns on hills ...rnings that ...panish ...da (a fleet ...med ships) ...pproaching ...ast, ready ...vasion. It took less than an ...for the message to travel ...s the length of the country.

------------------------------------ FOLLOW THE **HIGHWAY** ------►

2 Scientific messages

MESSAGE: "I AM THE SON OF GOD"

...esus Christ lived almost 2,000 years ...o in Palestine, in the Middle East. ...e Christian religion is based on his life ...d teachings.
...At the age of 30, Jesus began ...velling to preach his ideas about God ...d how people should live. He drew ...ge crowds wherever he went.
...Palestine's Roman rulers thought ...us' ideas would cause people to rebel. ...sus was arrested and executed.
...During his lifetime, Jesus' message was ...read by word of mouth. After his ...ath, his close followers, or disciples, ...ote down his teachings in the Bible.

MESSAGE: "ALL LIVING THINGS SHARE A FEW COMMON ANCESTORS"

✻ The British scientist Charles Darwin (1809-1882) is famous for his theory of evolution. This states that over millions of years all plants and animals have gradually developed from a few common ancestors.
✻ In 1859, Darwin published his ideas in a book, *The Origin of Species*. This shocked many people and caused fierce argument.
✻ Even today, not everyone agrees with Darwin's theory. Some people believe that God created all living things within a short period of time.

Visible Proof SPOT

Whisper a message into a friend's ear. They then whisper it to the next person, who whispers it to the next, and so on. The last person to receive the message reveals it to everyone. Is this message the same as the original one sent?

MESSAGES ARE NOT ALWAYS UNDERSTOOD THE WAY THEY WERE INTENDED...

✻ In 1945, during World War II, Japan replied to a message from the United States and its allies which asked it to surrender. The Japanese wanted more time, but their badly-worded answer wrongly suggested they would ignore the warning. Some people think this failed message partly led to the bombing of the Japanese cities of Hiroshima and Nagasaki.

22 Have communication advances made the world a better place?

Today, we are able to send messages quickly and in many different ways. We can easily share our knowledge and experience with others. But we need be aware of the possible consequences of our technological advances.

PRESERVING OUR DIFFERENCES

There is a risk of losing traditional means of communication if we all send messages in the same way.

THE YALI TRIBE

THEN Irian Jaya is the western half of the Pacific island of New Guinea. Parts of it are so remote that, until fairly recently, Europeans did not know anyone lived there. The Yali tribe live in the highlands of Irian Jaya, surrounded by dense tropical forests. The jungle has long shielded them from the outside world.

NOW The Yali language and culture is being threatened, as airports, satellite dishes and telephones start to appear along the coast.

THE NORTH AMERICAN INDIANS

As recently as 200 years ago, the North American Indians spoke more than 300 different languages. Today, only 40 or so are heard on any large scale. Most of the languages failed to survive because the few people who spoke them passed away, and because of the influence of American culture and the spread of English throughout the world.

FOLLOW THE HIGHWAY

23 What will happen to communication in the future?

From smoke signals and drum beats to cellular phones and the Internet – humans have always come up with more effective ways to get their messages across.

SCIENCE FICTION DREAMS?

In the future, we may evolve to such an extent that we can read each other's thoughts. We may be able to transport ourselves between places, simply by imagining it. These may appear far-fetched ideas – but so did walking on the Moon 100 years ago!

TINY TELEPHONES

Scientists are currently developing tiny telephones, which resemble the communicators used by the crew in the 1960s' television series *Star Trek*. The phones would be capable of sending and receiving both sound and pictures and may be worn as badges, bracelets or ear-rings.

HOLOGRAPHIC TELEVISIONS

Technologies are emerging that will allow very thin TV screens to be built. Future televisions will be hung up on walls like paintings, or even cover entire walls. Engineers are also working on holographic televisions, which use lasers to create three-dimensional images on-screen.

BYWAY TO SHOW ZONE 22

BYWAY TO SHOW ZONE 23

Visible Proof $\boxed{\text{SPOT}}$

...any of the Indian groups developed a ...mmon sign language so that they ...uld communicate with each other. ...vent a sign language ...your own and use it ...send messages to ...ur friends!

IS THERE ANYBODY OUT THERE?

...ving learnt how to send messages ...tween continents, we have now ...rned our attention to space. As part ...Project Phoenix – a worldwide search ...r alien life – huge radio telescopes are ...rgeting 200 stars for signals that ...uld have been made by intelligent ...e. Plaques on the sides of the Pioneer ...and 11 space probes carry images of ...ople and of the Earth's position in ...e solar system (see below).

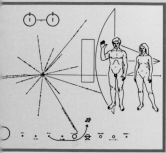

From the

Brain–

through space to the Impact Zone – you!

A journey that brings new ideas and discoveries, opinions and beliefs

Think!

From the first grunts to the Internet and intergalactic messages... what will the next 1,000 years bring?

Invisible Journeys
Communication
Index

✣ PICTURE CREDITS Front cover: left: Science Photo Library; centre: Telegraph Colour Library; right: Ace. Back cover: Zefa. P1 background: Astrid & Hans Frieder/Science Photo Library. P3 top: David Ducros/Jerrican/Science Photo Library; bottom: Pictor. P6 background: Tony Craddock/Science Photo Library; top, bottom: Scott Camazine/Science Photo Library. P7 background: Tony Craddock/Science Photo Library; bottom: Manfred Kage/Science Photo Library; top: Zefa. P8 left: CNRI/Science Photo Library; right: Rex Features. P9 top: Custom Medical Stock Photo/Science Photo Library; bottom: Retna. P10 Bruce Iverson/Science Photo Library. P11 Tony Stone. P12 top: Tony Stone; bottom: Ancient Art & Architecture (AA&A). P13 top: US Library of Congress/Science Photo Library; centre: Bridgeman Art Library; bottom: Rex Features. P14 top left: Sinclair Stammers/Science Photo Library; top right: AA&A; bottom left: Tony Stone. P15 top right: Brian Brake/Science Photo Library; bottom left: Tony Stone; bottom right: Science Photo Library. P16 top left: Mary Evans; top right: Library of Congress/Science Photo Library; bottom left: Pictor; bottom right: Advertising Archive. P17 top left, bottom right: Tony Stone; centre left, centre right: Science Photo Library; bottom centre: Harlequins Carnival/Joan Miró 1924-25 © ADAGP, Paris & DACS, London 1997/ Bridgeman Art Library. P18 background: Tony Craddock/Science Photo Library; top: Tony Stone; centre: AKG Photo; bottom left, bottom right: Mary Evans. P19 background: Tony Craddock/Science Photo Library; centre: Science & Society; bottom left: Zefa; bottom right: Rosenfeld Image Ltd/Science Photo Library. P21 top left: Science & Society; top centre bottom right: Mary Evans; top right: Science Photo Library; bottom right: Images; bottom centre: Tony Stone. P22 left: AA&A; right: Tony Stone. P24 top left, bottom right: Tony Stone; top right: Images; bottom centre: Pictor; bottom left: Zefa. P25 top: David Nunuk/Science Photo Library; bottom: Tony Stone. P26 background: Pictor; top: Allsport. P27 background, top centre: Pictor; top Left, bottom left: Tony Stone; right: Magnum Photos; bottom right: Camera Press. P28 top, bottom: AA&A. P29 top left, top centre: Hulton Getty; top right: Science & Society; bottom: AA&A; bottom centre: National Library of Medicine/Science Photo Library; bottom right: Popperfoto. P30 Tony Stone. P31 NASA/Science Photo Library.